AMAZING
MIGRATIONS

ICE

HARRIET BRUNDLE

©2018
Book Life
King's Lynn
Norfolk PE30 4LS

ISBN: 978-1-78637-224-6

All rights reserved
Printed in Malaysia

Written by:
Harriet Brundle

Edited by:
Kirsty Holmes

Designed by:
Gareth Liddington

A catalogue record for this book
is available from the British Library.

Photocredits: Abbreviations: l-left, r-right, b-bottom, t-top, c-centre, m-middle. All images are courtesy of Shutterstock.com.

CoverBg – Jo Crebbin, Covertl – Sylive Bouchard, Coverbl – David Boutin, 2 – Gecko1968. 4 – Roger Clark ARPS, 5t – FloridaStock, 5b – JoannaPe, 6tl – Joey_Danuphol, 6t – Pat Stornebrink, 6tr – outdoorsman, 6m – AndreAnita, 7t – Angela N Perryman, 7l – Nagel Photography, 7r – aquapix, 7bl – davemhuntphotography, 7br – pitcharee, 8 – wildestanimal, 9t – outdoorsman, 9b – MatsuKumi, 10 – Maksimilian, 11 – Mbz1, 13 – vladsilver, 14 – Vladimir Melnik, 15 – Joe Stone, 16 – Maksimilian, 17 – Mikhail Kolesnikov, 18 – outdoorsman, 19 – Art Babych, 20 – Thanapun, 21 – Jan Martin Will, 22t – KDdesignphoto, 22bl – Erni, 22br – evenfh, 23t – Vladimir Melnik, 23bl – evenfh, 23br – Rocks Antarc.

Images are courtesy of Shutterstock.com. With thanks to Getty Images, Thinkstock Photo and iStockphoto.

AMAZING MIGRATIONS

CONTENTS

Words that look like **this** can be found in the glossary on page 24.

The place where an animal lives is called its habitat. A good habitat has food, water and a safe place for an animal to raise their **young**.

Sea Ice

Although this polar bear lives on the ice, it spends its summers on land.

Tundra

There are many types of habitat and each one is different.

Animals live in habitats that meet their needs. Some habitats meet the needs of lots of different animals, so there will be different **species** living there.

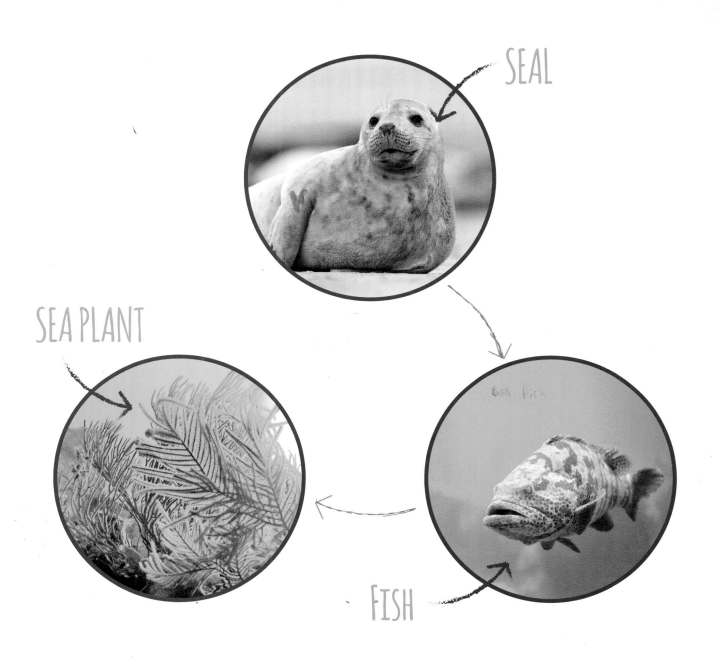

SEAL

SEA PLANT

FISH

Some habitats might have plants that animals can use for food or shelter. Some animals eat other animals in their habitat to **survive**. This is called a food chain.

WHAT DOES MIGRATION MEAN?

Migration is the movement of animals from one place to another. Some animals move small distances when they migrate while others travel hundreds of kilometres.

Some penguins walk over 280 kilometres to reach the sea.

Some animals that live on the ice migrate by swimming to another place. Others travel on top of the ice.

WHY DO ANIMALS MIGRATE?

Animals often migrate to find better **living conditions**. Food is often hard to find in an icy habitat, so animals migrate to other places to find more food.

Animals also migrate so that they can go on to lay eggs or to have young.

Penguins sit on their eggs to keep them warm!

EMPEROR PENGUINS

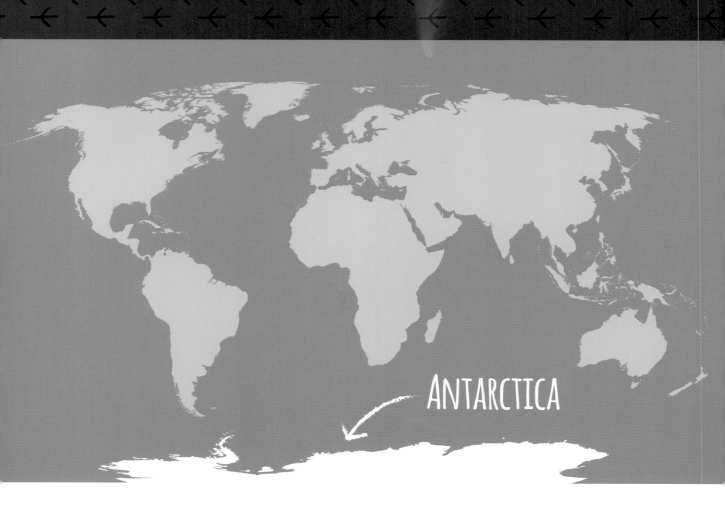

ANTARCTICA

Emperor penguins live in one of the coldest places on Earth: Antarctica. Every year, the penguins walk across the ice for many kilometres to reach a **breeding ground**.

Weeks later, the weather gets warmer and the ice starts to melt. The penguins and babies jump into the sea and swim away from the breeding ground.

HARP SEALS

Harp seals migrate from the **Arctic** to their birthing grounds, where they give birth to their young.

Seals are very good at **navigating** and can travel over 4,000 kilometres when they migrate.

Seals can stay underwater for 15 minutes at a time.

POLAR BEARS

Polar bears live on sea ice. In the warmer months, the ice melts away and the polar bears must migrate to spend summer on the land.

Tundra

Polar bears on the sea ice can catch food, such as seals.

When the temperature becomes colder again, the polar bears migrate back to the ice.

ARCTIC FOXES

Arctic foxes migrate to find **prey**. They eat small animals, which can be hard to find on the ice. The foxes travel long distances to find them.

Sometimes, the foxes follow polar bears across the sea ice so that they can eat their leftovers!

The Earth is becoming hotter over time because of something known as climate change. Climate change is causing **weather patterns** to change.

As the **temperature** gets warmer, the sea ice melts faster. This puts polar bears in danger because they have to stay on land longer, where it is hard to find food.

ACTIVITY

1. When emperor penguins make their migration over the ice, they often slide on their stomachs as they travel. Why do you think they do this?

2. The arctic fox has bright white fur for most of the year. Why do you think that might be?

3. Baby harp seals are born with fluffy white fur which they lose as they get older. Why do you think that might be?

4. Draw a picture of your favourite animal that lives on the ice. Add labels to give more information about your chosen animal.

GLOSSARY

Arctic
The area around the North Pole which is made up of the Arctic Ocean and the land surrounding it

breeding ground
an area where birds, fish and other animals go to breed

living conditions
the things that affect the way something lives

navigating
knowing to travel in a particular direction

prey
animals that are hunted by other animals for food

species
a group of very similar animals or plants that are able to produce young together

survive
continue to live

weather patterns
weather that we have become used to happening at particular times

young
an animal's offspring

INDEX